T0197549

Harry, My Dog

MARIAN KILER HALL

ILLUSTRATED BY: LYLE JAKOSALEM

To order additional copies of this book, contact:
Xlibris
1-888-795-4274
www.Xlibris.com
Orders@Xlibris.com

HARRY THE DOGGY

Harry, the Doggy, a happy dog is he,
Black and tan and white, a Basset Hound
Valerie and Roger, in my vacation spree,
Introduced Harry, the Doggy, to me.

His life had been hard for he was a stray,
Hungry and sore, with no place to stay.
Muddy and thin was this poor little pup.
Valerie said, "We'll soon fix you up."

We'll give you some water and give you some food,
A bath with some soap . You will soon feel good.
He must have a name. "What do you say?"
"Let's call him Harry." "Yes, Harry's OK."

Harry slept at their feet on their bed at night.
He roamed all about when it was light.
Val said, "Not good. He must stay in bounds,
He can't be allowed to run all around."

Roger said, "You're right. We must go and get
An electric fence to manage our pet."
They carefully surrounded most of the yard,
Establishing territory Harry would guard.

Harry soon learned the space had its thing;
When he ran out-of-bounds, he experienced a sting.
Harry was playful, a colorful sight.
He was loved by his owners, their favorite delight.

HARRY THE SWIMMER

Harry, the Swimmer, a happy dog is he,
Black and tan and white, a Basset Hound
The yard was huge and he could run
Around the house, it was such fun.

He rolled and stretched out in the grass,
But certain space he could not pass.
The clothesline that once made his day
Now was forbidden from his play.

That unseen fence had told him, "no"
Those clothes hung where he could not go.
There was a little swinging door
To enter the space with the tiled floor.

Which circled a full size swimming pool;
All screened in, it was sunny and cool.
When thirsty from playing, there he might drink.
How awful, one day, for before he could think.

12

He fell in the pool. It was nine feet deep.
Harry found he could swim, and that he could keep
His head above water. He awkwardly made
His way to the end, where, with steps as an aid.

He climbed out of the water, shook a minute or two
Before sunning himself on the tile. It's true;
Valerie witnessed the embarrassing scene.
She even told Roger all she had seen.

16

"Well, old boy," he said for what it is worth,
Maybe you'd better stick to the earth;
Don't play any hijinks at the swimming pools edge;
Drink where it's shallow and steps make a ledge.

"You can stand on the top step where it is not deep.
But mind you, be careful. Don't fall asleep."
Harry, the Swimmer, mended his ways.
He became Harry, the Doggy, every day.

HARRY GOODBYE

My vacation was short and I had to go,
But I really loved Harry, the doggy, and so
I patted his head and told him, "Be good".
Don't pull any pranks, but behave as you should.

TRAIN STATION

20

"Goodbye, Roger and Valerie. Bless you today.
You rescued Harry when he was a stray."
To the station we went, I got on the train
Minutes before there were oodles of rain.

I thought of the things that had happened to me –
I had met Harry, a dog you should see,
An adventurous doggy, but kind and true.
I am very glad that Harry met you.

Printed in the United States
By Bookmasters